cloverleaf books™

Nature's Patterns

When Will It Rain?

Noticing Weather Patterns

Martha E. H. Rustad

illustrated by Holli Conger

Ⓜ MILLBROOK PRESS · MINNEAPOLIS

For Sean and Emily,
from Auntie Martha —M.E.H.R.

For W & O, who always bring me
sunshine on rainy days —H.C.

Millbrook Press
A division of Lerner Publishing Group, Inc.
241 First Avenue North
Minneapolis, MN 55401 USA

For reading levels and more information, look up this title at
www.lernerbooks.com.

Main body text set in Slappy Inline 18/28.
Typeface provided by T26.

Library of Congress Cataloging-in-Publication Data

Rustad, Martha E. H. (Martha Elizabeth Hillman), 1975-
    When will it rain? : noticing weather patterns / by Martha
E. H. Rustad.
        pages   cm — (Cloverleaf books. Nature's patterns)
    Includes index.
    Audience: 005-008.
    Audience: K to Grade 3.
    ISBN 978-1-4677-8557-0 (lb : alk. paper) —
    ISBN 978-1-4677-8613-3 (pb : alk. paper) —
    ISBN 978-1-4677-8614-0 (eb pdf)
    1. Hurricanes—Juvenile literature. 2. Weather—Juvenile
literature. I. Title.
QC944.2.R86 2016
551.55'2—dc23   2014041021

Manufactured in the United States of America
1 – BP – 7/15/15

TABLE OF CONTENTS

Chapter One

How's the Weather?

"Good morning, class!" says Mr. Davis.

"Mr. Davis!" Katie giggles. "Why are you wearing a raincoat and boots?"

Our teacher smiles and says, "I'm going for a walk later."

"But look outside," says Praveen. "It's sunny and hot!"

"**Oops!**" Our teacher winks. "Guess I didn't check the forecast." Quinn asks what a forecast is. "**It's a weather prediction,**" Mr. Davis answers.

Forecasts can help you plan ahead. If the weather will be cold, wear a jacket. If rain is coming, pack an umbrella.

Our teacher tells us that we are starting a **weather project**. "Every day for the next month, we'll observe and record the weather," he says.

"What does *observe* mean?" Jamil asks.

"And *record*? Do you mean like a movie?" Samara wonders.

We learn that *observe* means "to look closely at something." *Record* means "to write down information."

Mr. Davis says, "Then we will look for **patterns.**"

"You mean things that happen over and over?" asks Daniel.

"Exactly," our teacher answers.

Scientists study weather patterns to see how climate changes. Climate is what the weather in one area is like over a long time.

Chapter Two

Weather Charts

Together, our class makes a chart to keep track of the **weather**. Then we go outside to see for ourselves. Is it **sunny** or **cloudy**? Is it **windy** or **calm**?

We look at the rain gauge. It measures precipitation.

We check the thermometer to record the temperature. We write down the temperature again before we go home later.

DATE	SKY (SUNNY / CLOUDY)	WIND	RAIN	TEMPERATURE Morning
				Afternoon

Rain and snow are different types of precipitation. So are hail, sleet, and drizzle!

The class looks at our chart after one week.
Lara raises her hand. "I see a **pattern**!
Afternoons are warmer than mornings."
Our teacher asks **why**.

"Maybe because the sun has been shining all
day!" Jameson answers. Mr. Davis nods.

"I see another **pattern!**" Katie says. "The days when it rained were cloudy."

"**Good observation,**" Mr. Davis says.

| DATE | SKY | | WIND | RAIN | TEMPERATURE | |
	SUNNY/CLOUDY				MORNING	AFTERNOON
Monday	Cloudy		Windy	0 in. (0 cm)	50°F (10°C)	65°F (18°C)
Tuesday	Cloudy		Calm	0.25 in. (.64 cm)	55°F (13°C)	70°F (21°C)
Wednesday	Sunny		Windy	0 in. (0 cm)	60°F (16°C)	65°F (18°C)
Thursday	Cloudy		Windy	1 in. (2.54 cm)	50°F (10°C)	55°F (13°C)
Friday	Sunny		Calm	0 in. (0 cm)	60°F (16°C)	75°F (24°C)

You can be a scientist! Being a scientist includes observing the world around you. Scientists also use their observations to make predictions.

We keep **observing** and **recording** the **weather**. After one month, we add up the amounts of rain that fell each day.

"Wow! Is 3 inches of rain a lot?" Samara asks.

"Let's look it up," Mr. Davis suggests.

We check precipitation totals for our town. We compare each month of the past year.

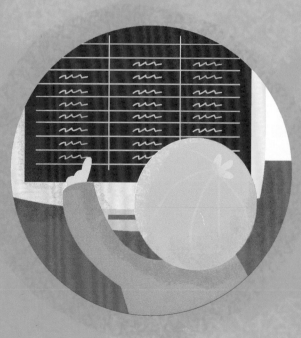

Month	Inches	Centimeters
January	0.5	1.3
February	0.5	1.3
March	1.5	3.8
April	2.5	6.4
May	3.0	7.6
June	1.5	3.8
July	0.5	1.3
August	0.5	1.3
September	1.0	2.5
October	1.5	3.8
November	2.5	6.4
December	0.5	1.3

"It looks like 3 inches is **a lot!**" our teacher says. We notice that our town gets more precipitation in spring and fall. Less rain or snow falls in summer and winter. That's another **pattern!**

Chapter Three

A Weather Visitor

"Today we have a surprise visitor!" Mr. Davis says. "Penny Perez is a meteorologist."

"She's on Channel 4!" Lara exclaims.

Daniel asks, "What's a meteorologist?"

Penny says, "I study **weather science**. I look at **patterns** and make weather predictions."

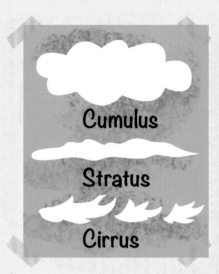

Cumulus

Stratus

Cirrus

"So you can tell the future?" Quinn asks.

"Not exactly," Penny laughs. "But I can tell you that tomorrow will be **rainy**."

Meteorologists go to college for at least four years after high school. They may work as weather forecasters for websites and radio or TV stations, or they may teach or do climate research.

Penny shows us tools that help her study the weather. "This barometer measures air pressure," she says. "High pressure brings **sunny, dry weather.** Low pressure often means **cool, wet weather.**"

Penny takes out a chart. It shows air pressure and rainfall. "Does anyone see a **pattern**?" she asks.

"Look! Rain falls on days with low pressure," Jameson notes.

"That's right. Today the air pressure is falling, so that means we'll have rain tomorrow," Penny says.

"Bummer," says Praveen. "Inside recess."

Air seems light, but it still weighs something. The weight of the air pressing down on Earth is called air pressure.

This Week's Air Pressure

Monday: High

Tuesday: Low

Wednesday: High

Thursday: High

Friday: Low

Our guest holds up another tool. "This is called an anemometer," she says. "It tells how fast the wind is blowing." Penny asks us to blow on it, like the wind. We act like we're blowing out birthday candles! We watch the cups spin quickly.

"Wow!" Penny winks. "Almost as fast as a hurricane."

"Can we really make a **hurricane**?" Jamil asks.
"No, hurricanes are huge storms, with winds that blow much faster than we can," Penny answers.

Hurricanes include strong winds and heavy rains. These spinning storms form over the ocean and can be 200 miles (322 kilometers) wide.

She says scientists learn about hurricanes by taking **measurements**. They record wind speed, temperature, and more. They look for **patterns** over time. "That helps them learn to make better forecasts to keep people safe," Penny says.

"Can you guess the most important **weather tool**?" Penny asks.

Daniel says, "Rain gauge?"

"Thermometer?" guesses Samara.

"**Your eyes!**" Penny answers. "Keep your eyes on the sky. Keep track and observe weather patterns."

It's time for Penny Perez to go. "What do we say to our guest?" our teacher asks.

"Can I have your autograph?" Lara asks.
Mr. Davis laughs and asks, "And what else?"

"Thank you!" we all say.

Make an Anemometer

Watch how fast the wind blows with your own anemometer.

You will need:

an adult to help

clay

a new pencil with a new eraser

two straight drinking straws

tape

four small plastic cups

a straight pin

1) Form the clay into a ball the size of a golf ball. Push the pencil straight up into it, but not all the way through it.

2) Push the clay down on a flat surface so one side flattens and the clay holds up the pencil.

3) Make an *X* with the straws and tape them together.

4) Tape one end of a straw to the side of each cup. Make sure the top rim of each cup faces the bottom of the next.

5) Push the straight pin through the middle of the *X* to attach the straws to the pencil eraser. Leave it loose enough that the straws can spin on the pin.

6) Place your anemometer outside and watch it spin. When it is still, no wind is blowing. The wind speed is low when it moves slowly. And when it spins quickly, watch out for a windy day!

GLOSSARY

air pressure: the weight of air on the surface of Earth

anemometer: a tool that measures wind speed

autograph: a famous person's signature

barometer: a tool that measures air pressure

climate: the weather in one place over a long period of time

forecast: a prediction of what will happen based on patterns and other information

hurricane: a large spinning storm with powerful winds of at least 74 miles (119 km) per hour

meteorologist: a scientist who studies weather

observe: to look closely at something

pattern: a repeated set of objects, traits, or events

precipitation: rain, snow, hail, or sleet

prediction: a thoughtful guess about what will happen

record: to write something down

temperature: how hot or cold something is

thermometer: a tool that measures temperature

weather: the state of the outside air, including temperature, precipitation, and wind, at a certain time and place

BOOKS

Boothroyd, Jennifer. *How Does Weather Change?* Minneapolis: Lerner Publications, 2015.
Learn more about the way weather changes daily.

Lawrence, Ellen. *What Is Climate? Weather Wise.* New York: Bearport, 2012.
Read about climates around the world.

WEBSITES

Kids Weather Report
http://kidsweatherreport.com
Find out the weather today and tomorrow.

Weather Underground
http://www.wunderground.com
Look up the weather history for your town.

Weather Watch
http://www.cyberbee.com/weatherwatch/
Record and share weather with other classes around the world.

LERNER ✎ SOURCE™

Expand learning beyond the printed book. Download free, complementary educational resources for this book from our website, www.lerneresource.com.